Sight-Word Mini-Books

Engaging Practice for Early Readers

by Keri King

A division of **Staff Development for EDUCATORS**

Peterborough, New Hampshire

Published by Crystal Springs Books
A division of Staff Development for Educators (SDE)
10 Sharon Road, PO Box 500
Peterborough, NH 03458
1-800-321-0401
www.crystalsprings.com
www.sde.com

© 2006 Keri King
Illustrations © 2006 Crystal Springs Books

Published 2006
Printed in the United States of America
10 09 08 07   3 4 5

ISBN-13: 978-1-884548-90-1
ISBN-10: 1-884548-90-3

Editor: Sharon Smith
Art Director, Designer, and Production Coordinator: Soosen Dunholter
Illustrator: Marci McAdam

Crystal Springs Books grants teachers the right to photocopy the reproducibles from this book for classroom use. No other part of this book may be reproduced in whole or in part, or stored in a retrieval system, or transmitted in any form or by any means, electronic, mechanical, photocopying, recording, or otherwise, without written permission of the publisher.

To all my students who love to read!

Contents

How to Use This Book 5
Assessment 8
Mini-Books 9

Book		Sight Word(s) Introduced	
1	I Like Food!	I, like	9
2	I Like the Farm.	the	11
3	I See the Zoo.	a, see	13
4	My Toys	my	15
5	I Like My School.	to	17
6	Go, Go, Go!	go	19
7	Things I Like!	and	21
8	Pets!	can	23
9	Yes, You Can!	you	25
10	Colors!	am	27
11	Rhyme Time!	on	29
12	On the Train!	is	31
13	At Night!	at	33
14	Who Is He?	he	35
15	Who Is She?	she	37
16	Look at the Bears!	look	39
17	The Weather	it	41
18	In the Water	in	43
19	Sports!	we	45
20	Look at This!	this	47
21	This Is Me!	me	49
22	What Do You Like?	do	51
23	Come to My Party!	come	53
24	Shapes!	here	55

How to Use This Book

Making the Books

1. Copy both pages of each mini-book. Set the copier to print the copies double sided, just as they appear in this book.

2. Cut each page into fourths.

3. Staple the pages of each book together, with the cover first and the list of included sight words last.

Using the Assessment Form

- Make one copy of the form per student.
- Pre-assess all students. Have each child read the sight words to you from the assessment form. Enter the date in the appropriate column and check off each word the child can read. Use this information to determine which mini-book the student should start with.
- Later in the year, at appropriate intervals, reassess each student, using the next column to check off the words the child can read.

Introducing the Mini-Books to Students

You will find the mini-books especially helpful as supplements to your guided-reading lessons. As you work with the books, you'll want to present them in order, so students read the easiest ones first and then build on what they've learned. Before students read each book, take a picture walk through the book with them. Discuss the pictures and story together and review the sight words on the back page of the book.

Areas of Student Growth Supported by the Mini-Books

In addition to reinforcing sight-word recognition, the books can also be useful in other ways. Use them to help students:

- develop directionality (reading from top to bottom and from left to right)
- attend to one-to-one correspondence
- use story patterns to develop fluency and expression
- use pictures to predict
- develop vocabulary
- use visual information to read new words
- use meaning to read new words
- self-correct when reading
- read independently
- build self-confidence

Other Activities That Help Build Sight-Word Mastery

Here are some additional sight-word strategies you might want to try in your classroom.

- Have students spell words with magnetic letters or letter tiles.
- Ask them to write words on whiteboards or in sand.
- Challenge them to find a few sight words in the book they're about to read.
- Have them build words with craft sticks, Play-Doh, etc.
- Have students use letter stamps to stamp out sight words.
- Put one sight word on each side of a block. Have the student roll the block and read each word as it comes up.
- Have students use highlighters to mark sight words in magazines.
- Make sight-word flash cards and let students play "Memory" or "Go Fish" with them.

_____'s Sight-Word Assessment

Date _____

Date				
I				
like				
the				
a				
see				
my				
to				
go				
and				
can				
you				
am				
on				
is				
at				

he				
she				
look				
it				
in				
we				
this				
me				
do				
come				
here				

Comments: _____
_____

I like pizza.

I Like Food!

I like watermelon.

I like carrots.

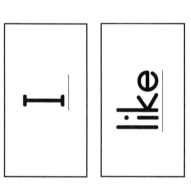

I like strawberries.

I
like

I like apples.

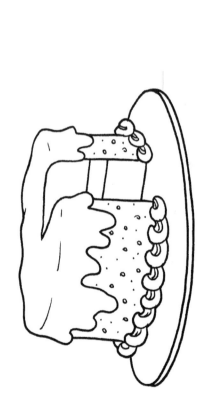

I like cake.

I Like the Farm.

I like the cow.

I like the sheep.

I like the pig.

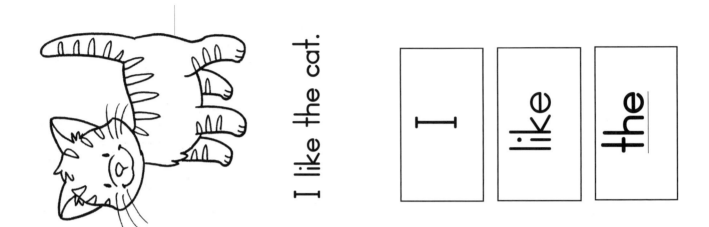

I like the cat.

| I | like | the |

I like the hen.

I like the duck.

I See the Zoo.

I see a giraffe.

I see the elephant.

I see monkeys.

I see a bear.

| I | a |
| the | see |

See the lion.

See the alligators.

My Toys

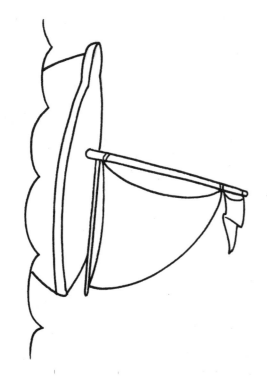

See my boat.

I see my doll.

I see my car.

I see my wagon.

I

see

my

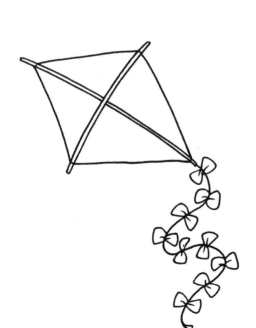

See my kite.

I see my bear.

I Like My School.

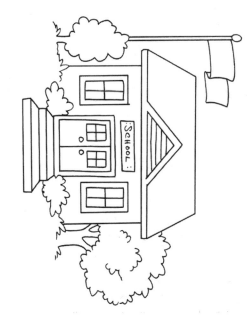

I like to read.

I like to sing.

I like my teacher.

I	like
my	to

I like to write.

I like to play.

I like my friends.

Go, Go, Go!

I like to go to school.

I go to the park.

I go to my house.

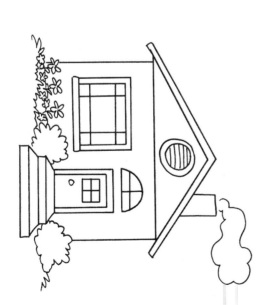

I go to the beach.

I	to
my	like
the	go

I like to go to parties.

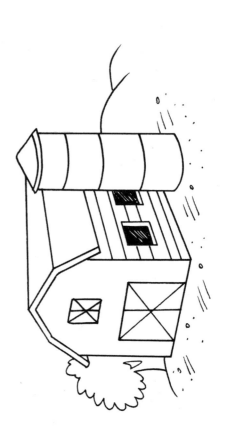

I like to go to the farm.

Things I Like!

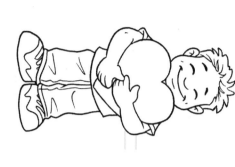

I like flowers and trees.

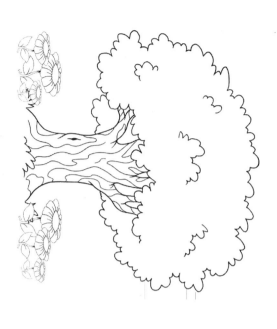

I like my trains and cars.

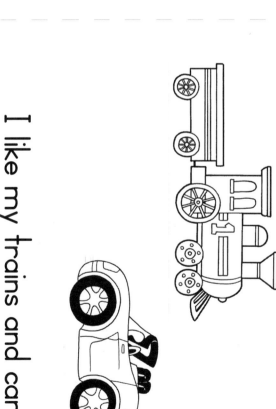

I like cats and dogs.

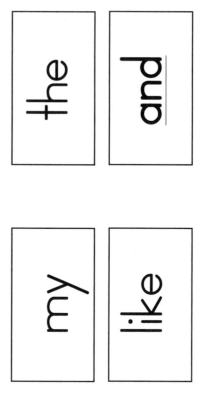

I like the moon and stars.

my	the
like	and

I like clowns and balloons.

I like my bat and ball.

Pets!

I can see my bunny.

Can I go see the snake?

The dog can see the bone.

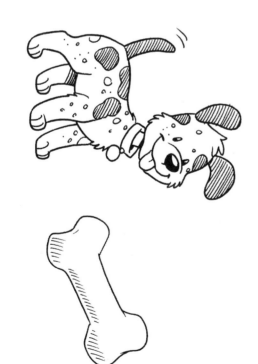

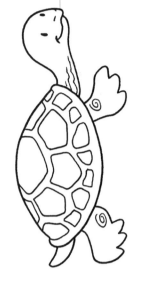

I can see my turtle.

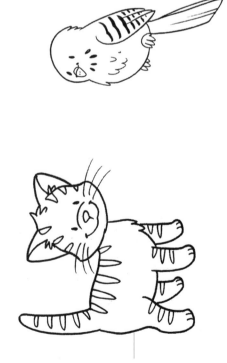

My cat can see the bird.

I can go see the fish.

my	go
see	I
the	can

Yes, You Can!

You can kick the ball.

You can dance!

Can you go swimming?

You can read the book!

can

you

a

the

go

Can you hit the ball?

You can write a letter.

Colors!

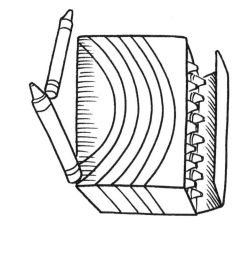

I am red. I am a heart.

I am green. I am a frog.

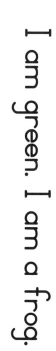

I am yellow. I am the sun.

I am pink. I am a flower.

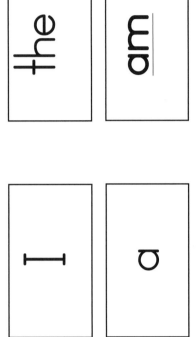

I	the
a	am

I am orange. I am a pumpkin.

I am black. I am a spider.

Rhyme Time!

Bug on the rug

Bee on the tree

Hat on my cat

Mouse on a house

the	on
a	my

Star on my car

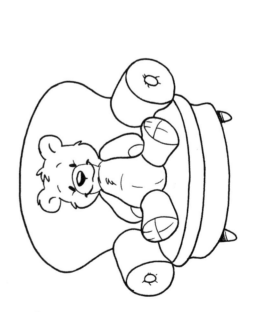

Bear on my chair

On the Train!

A bear is on the train.

My snake is on the train.

The alligator is on the train.

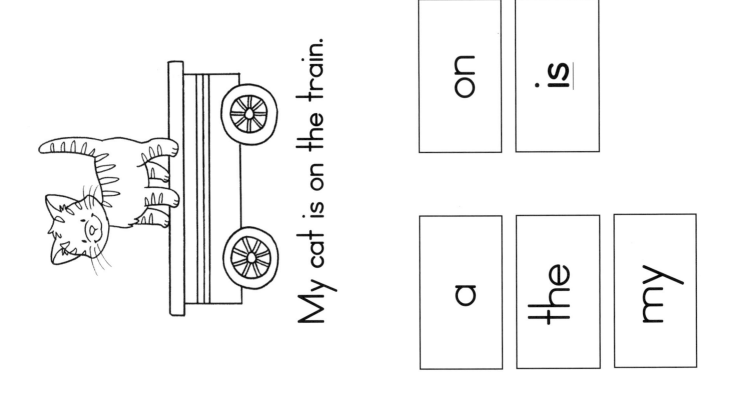

My cat is on the train.

| on | is |

| a | the | my |

Is a bird on the train?

Is a dog on the train?

At Night!

At night I can see stars.

Can you see a fox at night?

You can see owls at night.

At night I see raccoons.

At night I can see bats.

Can I see a skunk at night?

| see | at |

| a | you | can |

13

Who Is He?

He can cook!
He is my dad.

He likes baseball.
He is my friend.

He is on my skateboard.
He is my brother.

He is a toy!
He is my robot.

my		can
likes		on
he		is

14

He likes to write.
He is my grandpa.

He likes bones!
He is my dog.

Who Is She?

She is a pet.
She is my cat.

She likes to read.
She is my mom.

She is nice.
She is my grandma.

She likes to write!
She is my teacher.

She is a toy.
She is my doll.

She can swim!
She is my sister.

to	can
likes	my
she	is

15

Look at the Bears!

Look at the bear!
He is writing.

Look! A bear!
She likes cookies.

Look at my bear.
He is running.

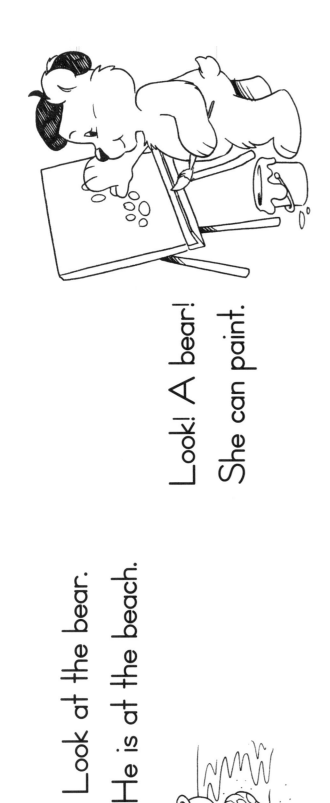

Look! A bear!
She can paint.

Look at the bear.
He is at the beach.

can	she
at	he
look	is

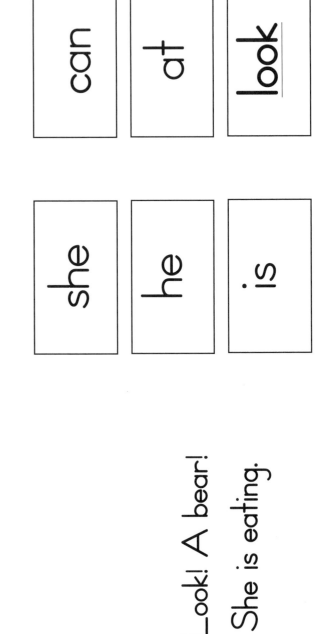

Look! A bear!
She is eating.

The Weather

Look! It is snowing!

It is raining.

Is it windy?

It is cloudy.

It is sunny and hot!

Look! It is a rainbow!

is	it
and	look

In the Water

Look! A frog is in the water!

I see a turtle in the water.

A fish is in the water.

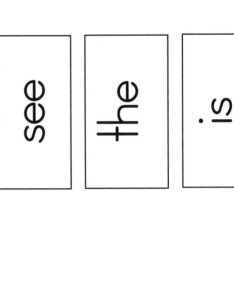

Is the duck in the water?

see	my
the	look
is	in

Is my boat in the water?

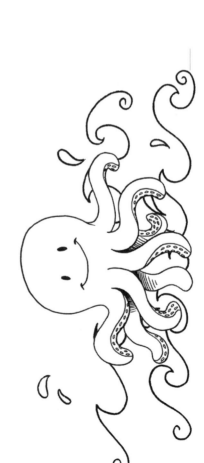

The octopus is in the water!

18

Sports!

We can play baseball.
I can hit the ball.

We can play basketball.
I like to shoot.

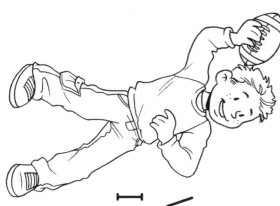

We can play football.
I am the quarterback.

We can go play soccer.
I can kick the ball.

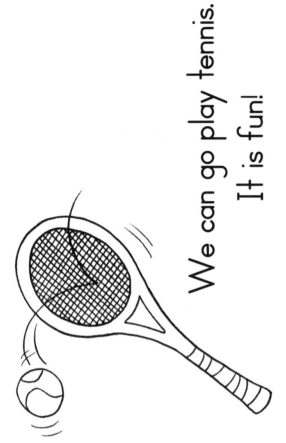

We can go play tennis.
It is fun!

I		is
can		it
we		go

We can play volleyball.
I like to win!

Look at This!

Look! This is my cat! She is soft.

Look! This is a snake. It is long!

This is a mouse. He is small.

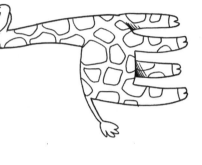

Look! This is a giraffe. She is tall.

Look! This is a snail. He is slow.

can	look	this
she	he	is

20

This is a butterfly! It can fly.

This Is Me!

This is me! I am a cook.

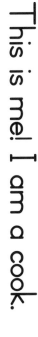

This is me! I am a student.

This is me! I am a cheerleader.

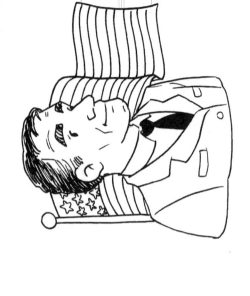

This is me! I am the President.

is	am
a	this
the	me

21

This is me! I am a farmer.

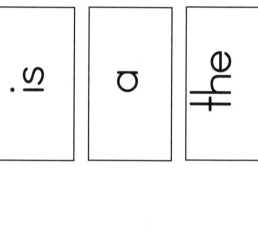

This is me! I am a singer.

What Do You Like?

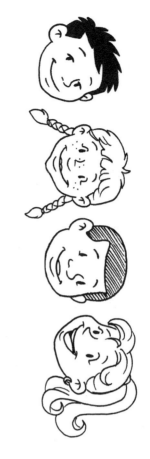

Do you see the paint?
Do you like to paint?

Do you see the guitar?
Do you like music?

Do you like the computer?
Do you play on it?

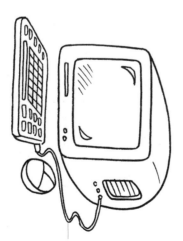

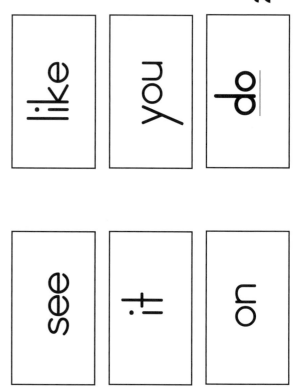

Do you go to school?
Do you ride the bus?

Do you see the plane?
Do you like to fly?

Do you see the books?
Do you like to read?

see	like
it	you
on	do

Come to My Party!

Come and see my friends.
We can play!

Come in my house!

Come and see the clown.
He is funny!

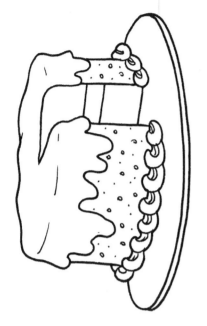

Come and eat the cake.
It is big!

Come and see my balloon.
It is a heart.

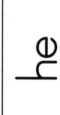

Come and look at my bear.
It is a present.

look	he
at	it
<u>come</u>	we

Shapes!

Here is a triangle!
Do you like pizza?

Here is a circle.
It is a balloon.

Here is a square!
It is a present.

Here is a diamond.
Come and see the kite.

you	look
do	this
come	here

Here is a rectangle.
Look at this book!

Here is an oval.
Look! It is an egg!

24